SESAME STREET
123

Keep TRYING

with Abby

A Book about Persistence

Jill Colella

Lerner Publications ◆ Minneapolis

Sesame Street's mission has always been about teaching kids much more than simply the ABCs and 123s. This series of books about nurturing the positive character traits of generosity, respect, empathy, positive thinking, resilience, and persistence will help children grow into the best versions of themselves. So come along with your funny, furry friends from Sesame Street as they learn about making themselves—and the world—smarter, stronger, and kinder.

—Sincerely, the Editors at Sesame Street

TABLE OF CONTENTS

What Is Persistence?

Sometimes we don't get something right on the first try.

I don't get all my magic right, but I keep trying!

Persistence means not giving up!

Keep Trying!

Doing something new can feel scary.
But new things help us grow.

When did you try something new?

Maybe you can't do something . . . yet.

Break big goals into small steps.
Think of getting dressed.

What is another task that you can break into parts?

First, you put on your shirt, then pants, and then socks.

13

If you can't do something at first, make a new plan.

Think about a time you solved a problem. What did you do?

Try solving a problem in a different way.

Our parents, teachers, and friends care about us. They can help us reach our goals.

I skate slowly and hold Ernie's hand. I can't go fast—yet!

When we keep trying, we can master new skills. That makes us feel good!

Elmo learned the ABCs and how each letter sounds. Now Elmo loves to read!

Persistence helps us focus,
practice, and keep trying!

BE A BUDDY!

With a friend, build a tall block tower. If it falls over, try again. Talk about different ways to make your tower strong.

Glossary

different: not in the same way

focus: pay a lot of attention to

goal: something you want to do

master: become very good at

Learn More

Bushman, Susanne M. *Don't Give Up.* Minneapolis: Jump!, 2020.

Colella, Jill. *Bouncing Back with Big Bird: A Book about Resilience.* Minneapolis: Lerner Publications, 2021.

Schuh, Mari. *Yes I Can! A Story of Grit.* Minneapolis: Millbrook Press, 2018.

Index

Photo Acknowledgments

Additional image credits: GUNDAM_Ai/Shutterstock.com, p. 4; Denis Kuvaev/Shutterstock.com, p. 5; Anna Om/Shutterstock.com, p. 6; Studio 1One/Shutterstock.com, p. 7; Dmytro Vietrov/Shutterstock.com, pp. 8, 9; Rawpixel.com/Shutterstock.com, p. 10; Purino/Shutterstock.com, p. 11; myboys.me/Shutterstock.com, p. 12; Krakenimages.com/Shutterstock.com, p. 13; Evgeny Atamanenko/Shutterstock.com, p. 14; KK Tan/Shutterstock.com, p. 15; Kathy Matsunami/Shutterstock.com, p. 16; Daniel Chetroni/Shutterstock.com, p. 17; Alexandru Marian/Shutterstock.com, p. 18; Tomsickova Tatyana/Shutterstock.com, p. 19; TORWAISTUDIO/Shutterstock.com, p. 20.

For the girls: LKAT, PKAT, and EVAF

Lerner Publications Company
An imprint of Lerner Publishing Group, Inc.
241 First Avenue North
Minneapolis, MN 55401 USA

For reading levels and more information, look up this title at www.lernerbooks.com.

Main body text set in Billy Infant. Typeface provided by SparkyType.

Editor: Alison Lorenz **Designer:** Emily Harris **Photo Editor:** Brianna Kaiser **Lerner team:** Sue Marquis

Library of Congress Cataloging-in-Publication Data

Names: Colella, Jill, author.
Title: Keep trying with Abby : a book about persistence / Jill Colella.
Description: Minneapolis : Lerner Publications, 2021. | Series: Sesame street ® character guides | Includes bibliographical references and index. | Audience: Ages 4–8 | Audience: Grades K-1 | Summary: "Being persistent means not giving up! Abby and the gang from Sesame Street help kids learn they can solve problems and make mistakes as long as they keep trying"—Provided by publisher.
Identifiers: LCCN 2020009435 (print) | LCCN 2020009436 (ebook) | ISBN 9781728403922 (library binding) | ISBN 9781728418728 (ebook)
Subjects: LCSH: Persistence—Juvenile literature. | Self-realization—Juvenile literature.
Classification: LCC BF637.S4 C6525 2021 (print) | LCC BF637.S4 (ebook) | DDC 158.1—dc23

LC record available at https://lccn.loc.gov/2020009435
LC ebook record available at https://lccn.loc.gov/2020009436

Manufactured in the United States of America
1-48392-48906-5/29/2020